Greta,

To a nice person I
enjoy talking to at
the dog park.

Toytraindoc
Raycho
9/25/15

Toy Train Doc's
Train Show Parts
QUICK REFERENCE GUIDE

by Ralpho

Steamers, Diesels, Motor Accessories

authorHOUSE®

AuthorHouse™
1663 Liberty Drive, Suite 200
Bloomington, IN 47403
www.authorhouse.com
Phone: 1-800-839-8640

First published by AuthorHouse 2/25/2008

ISBN: 978-1-4343-5200-2 (sc)

Library of Congress Control Number: 2008901584

Printed in the United States of America
Bloomington, Indiana

This book is printed on acid-free paper.

Acknowledgements

The Ofchinick Family (Gloria, Eric and Marc), for their many years of patience while this data was being developed

Contents

CHAPTER SIX

Locomotives 34

CHAPTER SEVEN

Scout. 42

CHAPTER EIGHT

General 46

CHAPTER ELEVEN

Fairbank Morse Diesel. 58

CHAPTER TWELVE

GP7 - GP9 Diesel. 62

CHAPTER THIRTEEN

Rectifier Electric. 66

CHAPTER FOURTEEN

Locomatives 74

CHAPTER FIFTHTEEN

Whistle. 78

CHAPTER ONE
SWITCHERS

	UNIT #	Year	Tender #	Motor #	Brush #
Alco - Union Pacific	202	57	N/A	N/A	622-121
Alco - Sante Fe	204	57	N/A	N/A	622-121
Alco - Missouri Pacific	205	57	N/A	N/A	622-121
					622-121
Alco - Sante Fe	208	58	N/A	N/A	1055-136
					622-121
Alco - New Haven	209	58	N/A	N/A	1055-136
					622-121
Alco - Texas Special	210	58	N/A	N/A	1055-136
					622-121
Alco - US. Marine	212	58	N/A	N/A	1055-136
					622-121
Alco - Burlington	216	58	N/A	N/A	1055-136
					622-121
Alco - Boston & Maine	217	59	N/A	N/A	1055-136

UNIT #		Spring #	Bulb #	Volts	Roller #
Alco - Union Pacific	202	622-191	53	12-16	2328-95
Alco - Sante Fe	204	622-191	53	12-16	2328-95
Alco - Missouri Pacific	205	622-191	53	12-16	2328-95
Alco - Sante Fe	208	622-191	57	12-16	2328-95
Alco - New Haven	209	622-191	57	12-16	2328-95
Alco - Texas Special	210	622-191	57	12-16	2328-95
Alco - US. Marine	212	622-191	57	12-16	2328-95
Alco - Burlington	216	622-191	57	12-16	2328-95
Alco - Boston & Maine	217	622-191	57	12-16	2328-95

	UNIT #	E-Unit	Smoke	Power Truck #
Alco - Union Pacific	202	101-1	N/A	202-117
Alco - Sante Fe	204	100-11	N/A	218-101
Alco - Missouri Pacific	205	100-11	N/A	204-101
Alco - Sante Fe	208	100-11	N/A	204-101
Alco - New Haven	209	100-11	N/A	204-101
		100-11		
Alco - Texas Special	210	101-1	N/A	204-101
Alco - US. Marine	212	101-1	N/A	202-107
Alco - Burlington	216	100-11	N/A	204-101
Alco - Boston & Maine	217	100-11	N/A	204-101

CHAPTER TWO
200 Series ALCOS

	UNIT #	Year	Tender #	Motor #	Brush #
Alco - Union Pacific	202	57	N/A	N/A	622-121
Alco - Sante Fe	204	57	N/A	N/A	622-121
Alco - Missouri Pacific	205	57	N/A	N/A	622-121
Alco - Sante Fe	208	58	N/A	N/A	622-121 1055-136
Alco - New Haven	209	58	N/A	N/A	622-121 1055-136
Alco - Texas Special	210	58	N/A	N/A	622-121 1055-136
Alco - US. Marine	212	58	N/A	N/A	622-121 1055-136
Alco - Burlington	216	58	N/A	N/A	622-121 1055-136
Alco - Boston & Maine	217	59	N/A	N/A	622-121 1055-136

	UNIT #	Roller #	Smoke	Power Truck #
Alco - Union Pacific	202	2328-95	N/A	202-117
Alco - Sante Fe	204	2328-95	N/A	218-101
Alco - Missouri Pacific	205	2328-95	N/A	204-101
Alco - Sante Fe	208	2328-95	N/A	204-101
Alco - New Haven	209	2328-95	N/A	204-101
Alco - Texas Special	210	2328-95	N/A	204-101
Alco - US. Marine	212	2328-95	N/A	202-107
Alco - Burlington	216	2328-95	N/A	204-101
Alco - Boston & Maine	217	2328-95	N/A	204-101

	UNIT #	Spring #	E-Unit	Bulb #	Volts
Alco - Union Pacific	202	622-191	101-1	53	12-16
Alco - Sante Fe	204	622-191	100-11	53	12-16
Alco - Missouri Pacific	205	622-191	100-11	53	12-16
Alco - Sante Fe	208	622-191	100-11	57	12-16
Alco - New Haven	209	622-191	100-11	57	12-16
Alco - Texas Special			100-11		
	210	622-191	101-1	57	12-16
Alco - US. Marine	212	622-191	101-1	57	12-16
Alco - Burlington	216	622-191	100-11	57	12-16
Alco - Boston & Maine	217	622-191	100-11	57	12-16

UNIT #		Spring #	Bulb #	Volts	Roller #
Alco - Sante Fe	218	622-191	57	12-16	2328-95
Alco - Missouri Pacific	219	622-191	57	12-16	2328-95
Alco - Sante Fe	220	622-191	57	12-16	2328-95
Alco - US. Navy	224	622-191	57	12-16	2328-95
Alco - Chesapeake & Ohio	225	622-191	57	12-16	2328-95
Alco - Boston & Maine	226	622-191	53	12-16	2328-95
Alco - Canadian National	227	622-191	53	12-16	2328-95
Alco - Canadian National	228	622-191	53	12-16	2328-95
Alco - Minneapolis & St. Louis	229	622-191	53	12-16	2328-95
Alco - Chesapeake & Ohio	230	622-191	53	12-16	2328-95
Alco - Rock Island	231	622-191	53	12-16	2328-95
Alco - Texas Special	1055	622-191	53	12-16	2328-95
Alco - Union Pacific	1065	622-191	53	12-16	2328-95

	UNIT #	E-Unit	Smoke	Power Truck #
Alco - Sante Fe	218	100-11	N/A	218-101
Alco - Missouri Pacific	219	101-1	N/A	219-101
Alco - Sante Fe	220	100-11	N/A	204-101
Alco - US. Navy	224	100-11	N/A	204-101
Alco - Chesapeake & Ohio	225	101-1	N/A	204-101
Alco - Boston & Maine	226	100-11	N/A	204-101
Alco - Canadian National	227	101-1	N/A	204-101
Alco - Canadian National	228	100-11	N/A	204-101
Alco - Minneapolis & St. Louis	229	101-1	N/A	229-101
Alco - Chesapeake & Ohio	230	101-1	N/A	204-101
Alco - Rock Island	231	101-1 / 101-1	N/A	204-101
Alco - Texas Special	1055	100-11 / 101-1	N/A	1055-101
Alco - Union Pacific	1065	100-11	N/A	204-101

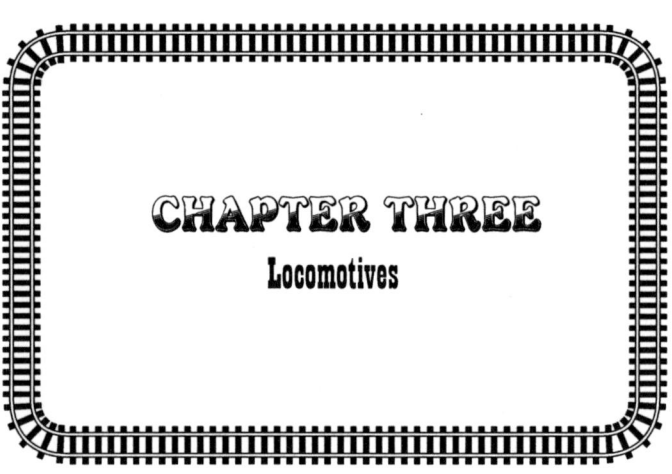

CHAPTER THREE

Locomotives

	UNIT #	Year	Tender #	Motor #	Brush #
Hudson	221	47	221W	221m-1	166-129
			221T		
			2466W		
			2466T		
Prairie	224		2466WX	2.24E-23	166-129
			233W		
Plastic	233	61	243W	233-100	246-295
			1060T		
Plastic	235	61	1130T	236-100	246-295
			1130T		
Plastic	236	61	1050T	236-100	246-295
			1060T		
Plastic	245	59	1130T	245-100	246-295
			1131T		
Plastic	246	59	244T	246-200	246-295
Metal Scout	249	58	250T	249-100	622-121
Metal Scout	250	57	250T	250-100	622-121

Notes:

UNIT #	Spring #	Bulb #	Volts	Roller #
Hudson 221	224E-101	430	14	1661-33
Prairie 224	224E-101	430	14	Shoe
Plastic 233	246-212	51	6-8	SLS-254-3
Plastic 235	246-212	51	6-8	246-105
Plastic 236	246-212	51	6-8	246-105
Plastic 245	246-212	51	6-8	246-105
Plastic 245	246-212	51	6-8	246-105
Plastic 246	246-212	51	6-8	246-105
Metal Scout 249	2036-157	51	6-8	246-105
Metal Scout 250	2036-157	51	6-8	246-105

	UNIT #	E-Unit	Smoke	Power Truck #
Hudson	221	226E-35	N/A	-
Prairie	224	226E-35	N/A	-
Plastic	233	Pawl	233-50	-
Plastic	235	Pawl	N/A	-
Plastic	236	Pawl	236-50	-
Plastic	245	Pawl	N/A	-
Plastic	246	Pawl	N/A	-
Metal Scout	249	100-2	N/A	-
Metal Scout	250	100-2	N/A	-

CHAPTER FOUR
Diesel Cars

	UNIT #	Year	Tender #	Motor #	Brush #
Budd Car	400	56	N/A	N/A	622-121
Budd Car	404	57	N/A	N/A	622-121

Notes:

Notes:

UNIT #	Spring #	Bulb #	Volts	Roller #
Budd Car 400	622-191	57	6-8	246-105
Budd Car 404	622-191	57	6-8	246-105

	UNIT #	E-Unit	Smoke	Truck #
Budd Car	400	100-4	N/A	2028-100
Budd Car	404	100-14	N/A	2028-100

Notes:

CHAPTER FIVE
EMD Switchers

UNIT #	Year	Tender #	Motor #	Brush #
EMD NW-2	600	55	N/A	N/A	622-121
EMD NW-2	610	55	N/A	N/A	622-121
EMD NW-2	601	56	N/A	N/A	622-121
EMD NW-2	621	56	N/A	N/A	622-121
EMD NW-2	602	57	N/A	N/A	622-121
EMD NW-2	611	57	N/A	N/A	622-121
EMD NW-2	613	58	N/A	N/A	622-121
EMD NW-2	616	61	N/A	N/A	622-121
EMD NW-2	614	59	N/A	N/A	622-121
EMD NW-2	622	49	N/A	622-100	622-121
EMD NW-2	622	50	N/A	622-100	622-121
EMD NW-2	6220	49	N/A	622-100	622-121
EMD NW-2	6220	50	N/A	622-100	622-121
EMD NW-2	633	50	N/A	N/A	622-121

UNIT #	Spring #	Bulb #	Volts	Roller #
EMD NW-2	600	622-191	N/A	N/A	2328-92
EMD NW-2	610	622-191	N/A	N/A	2328-92
EMD NW-2	601	622-191	N/A	N/A	2328-92
EMD NW-2	621	622-191	N/A	N/A	2328-92
EMD NW-2	602	622-191	53	12-16	2328-92
EMD NW-2	611	622-191	53	12-16	2328-92
EMD NW-2	613	622-191	53	12-16	2328-92
EMD NW-2	616	622-191	53	12-16	2328-92
EMD NW-2	614	622-191	53	12-16	2328-92
EMD NW-2	622	622-191	363	14	622-55
EMD NW-2	622	622-118	363	14	2333-36
EMD NW-2	6220	622-118	363	14	622-55
EMD NW-2	6220	622-118	363	14	2023-43
EMD NW-2	633	622-191	363	14	2328-92

UNIT #		E-Unit	Smoke	Power Truck #
EMD NW-2	600	100-14	N/A	601-101
EMD NW-2	610	100-14	N/A	601-101
EMD NW-2	601	100-14	N/A	601-101
EMD NW-2	621	100-14	N/A	621-101
EMD NW-2	602	100-14	N/A	601-101
EMD NW-2	611	100-14	N/A	601-101
EMD NW-2	613	100-14	N/A	601-101
EMD NW-2	616	100-14	N/A	601-101
EMD NW-2	614	101-3	N/A	614-101
EMD NW-2	622	100-20	N/A	-
EMD NW-2	622	100-20	N/A	-
EMD NW-2	6220	100-20	N/A	-
EMD NW-2	6220	100-20	N/A	-
EMD NW-2	633	100-19	N/A	621-101 601-101

CHAPTER SIX

Locomotives

UNIT #		Year	Tender #	Motor #	Brush #
Hudson	665	54	736W 2046W 6026W	2035-100 2025-100	226E-92
Hudson	685	53	2046W 6026W	2025-100 2035-100	226E-92
Hudson	2055	53	2046W	2025-100 2035-100	226E-92
Hudson	2065	54	2046W 6026W	2025-100 2035-100	226E-92
Turbin	671	46	671W 2671W 2020W 2466W	671M-1	2020M-33
Turbin	2020	46	6020W	671M-1	2020M-33

Notes:

UNIT #	Spring #	Bulb #	Volts	Roller #
Hudson 665	2036-157	57	12-16	SLS-254-3
Hudson 685	2036-157	57	12-16	SLS-254-3
Hudson 2055	2036-157	57	12-16	SLS-254-3
Hudson 2065	2036-157	57	12-16	SLS-254-3
Turbin 671	2020M-34	1447	18	671-105
Turbin 2020	2020M-34	1447	18	671-105

	UNIT #	E-Unit	Smoke	Power Truck #
Hudson	665	100-25	675-9	-
Hudson	685	100-25	675-9	-
Hudson	2055	100-25	675-9	-
Hudson	2065	100-25	675-9	-
Turbin	671	671-90	671-170	-
Turbin	2020	671-90	671-170	-

UNIT #	Year	Tender #	Motor #	Brush #
Turbin 671R	46	4424W 4671W 2466WX	671M-1	2020M-33
K4-Pacific 675	47-49	2466T 6466WX 2046W 2466W	671M-1	2020M-33
K4-Pacific 2025	47-49	2466WX 6466W	671M-1	2020M-33
Berkshire 726	46	2426W	726M-1	2020M-33
Berkshire 726	47-49	2046W	671M-1	2020M-33
Hudson 736	50	2671WX	681-100	622-100
Northern - J 746	57	746W 2426W 736W	681-100	622-100
Hudson 773	50	773W	773-200	622-100

UNIT #	Spring #	E-Unit	Bulb #	Volts
Turbin	671R	2020M-34	671-90	1447	18
K4-Pacific	675	2020M-34	671-90	1447	18
K4-Pacific	2025	2020M-34	671-90	1447	18
Berkshire	726	2020M-34	726-51	799 (S)	18
Berkshire	726	2020M-34	726-90	1447	18
Hudson	736	622-191	100-25	1447	18
Northern - J	746	622-191	100-25	19	14
Hudson	773	622-191	733-300	1447	18

UNIT #	Roller #	Smoke	Power Truck #
Turbin 671R	671-105	671-170	-
K4-Pacific 675	671-105	671-170	-
K4-Pacific 2025	671-105	671-170	-
Berkshire 726	671-111	799 (S)	-
Berkshire 726	671-111	799 (S)	-
Hudson 736	681-15	671-170	-
Northern - J 746	2328-95	746-60	-
Hudson 773	681-16	671-170	-

Notes:

CHAPTER SEVEN
Scout

	UNIT #	Year	Tender #	Motor #	Brush #
Plastic	1001	48	1001T	1001M-1	622-121
Plastic	1050	59	1050T	1050-100	622-121
			1050T		
Plastic	1060	60-62	1060T	1050-200	1001M-46
Plastic	1110	49-50	1001T	1110-50	296-211
Plastic	1110	51-52	1001T	2034-100	246-211
Plastic	1120	50	1001T	1120-100	1001M-46
Plastic	6110	50	6001T	6110-100	1001M-46
Metal Scout	1615	55	1615T	1615-100	622-121
			1654T		
	1654	46-47	1654W	1654M-1	1-92
			1654T		
Alco	1655	48	1654W	1654M-1	1-92
Alco	1656	48	2304B	1656M-1	1-92

UNIT #	Spring #	E-Unit	Bulb #	Volts
Plastic 1001	1001M-1	Pawl	51	6-8
Plastic 1050	246-212	Pawl	51	6-8
Plastic 1060	246-212	Pawl	51	6-8
Plastic 1110	1001M-47	Pawl	51	6-8
Plastic 1110	1001M-47	Pawl	51	6-8
Plastic 1120	1001M-47	Pawl	N/A	
Plastic 6110	1001M-47	Pawl	N/A	
Metal Scout 1615	2036-157	100-3	57	12-16
Alco 1654	OM-22	226E-33	430	14
Alco 1655	OM-22	226E-33	430	14
Alco 1656	OM-22	226E-33	430	14

	UNIT #	Roller #	Smoke	Power Truck #
Plastic	1001	1001M-6	N/A	-
Plastic	1050	246-105	233-50	-
Plastic	1060	246-105	236-50	-
Plastic	1110	246-105	N/A	-
Plastic	1110	1001M-6	N/A	-
Plastic	1120	1001M-6	N/A	-
Plastic	6110	1001M-6	6110-15	-
Metal Scout	1615	2036-125	N/A	-
	1654	1661-35 Shoe	N/A	-
Alco	1655	1661-35 Shoe	N/A	-
Alco	1656	1661-35 Shoe	N/A	-

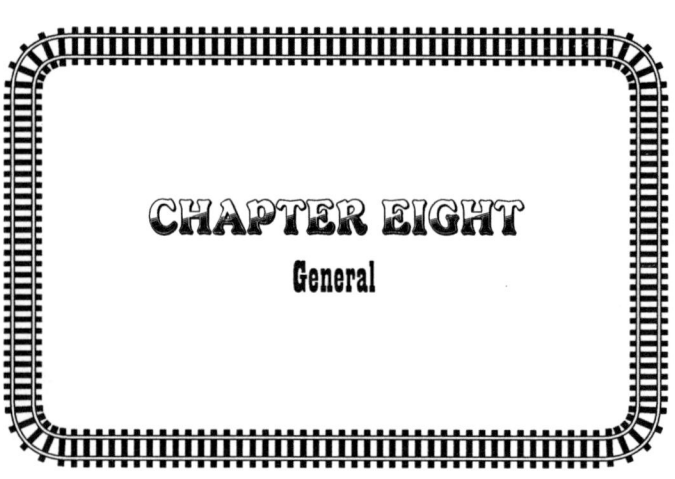

CHAPTER EIGHT
General

UNIT #		Year	Tender #	Motor #	Brush #
General	1862	59	1862T		622-121
			1875W	1862-100	1055-136
General	1872	59	1872T		622-121
			1875W	1872-100	1055-136
General	1882		1882T		
			1875W		

Notes:

Notes:

UNIT #	Spring #	Bulb #	Volts	Roller #
General 1862	622-191	191	16	1862-97
General 1872	622-191	191	16	1862-97
General 1882				1862-97

	UNIT #	E-Unit	Smoke	Power Truck #
General	1862	101-4	N/A	-
General	1872	100-12	N/A	-
General	1882			-

Notes:

CHAPTER NINE
Diesel

	UNIT #	Year	Tender #	Motor #	Brush #
Alco	2023	50	N/A	2023-100	622-121
			6466W		
			6466T		
			6066T		
Mid Size	2026	51-53	6466WX	2026M-1	1661E-29
Metal Scout	2034	52	6066T	2034-100	226E-92
			1130T		
Metal Scout	1130	53	6066T	2034-100	226E-92
K4-Pacific	2035	52	6466W	2035-100	226E-92
K4-Pacific	2035	51	6466W	2035-100	226E-92
			2466WX		
			6466WX		
K4-Pacific	2025	52	6466W	2025-100	226E-92

UNIT #	Spring #	Bulb #	Volts	Roller #
Alco 2023	622-191	363	14	2023-43
				1661-23
Mid Size 2026	224E-101	1445	18	Shoe
Metal Scout 2034	2036-157	363	14	2036-122
Metal Scout 1130	2036-157	263	14	2036-122
K4-Pacific 2035	2036-157	1447	18	SLS-254-3
K4-Pacific 2035	2036-157	1447	18	2035-140
K4-Pacific 2025	2036-157	1447	18	2035-140

	UNIT #	E-Unit	Smoke	Power Truck #
Alco	2023	100-15	N/A	-
Mid Size	2026	226E-35	2026-8	-
Metal Scout	2034	100-2	N/A	-
Metal Scout	1130	100-2	N/A	-
K4-Pacific	2035	100-2	671-167 / 675-9	-
K4-Pacific	2035	100-2	671-167 / 675-9	-
K4-Pacific	2025	100-2	671-167 / 675-9	-

CHAPTER TEN
2300 Series

	UNIT #	Year	Tender #	Motor #	Brush #
GM F3	2363	53	N/A	2026-100	622-121
GM F3	2368	55	N/A	2026-100	622-121
GM F3	2373	57	N/A	2026-100	622-121
GM F3	2378	55	N/A	2026-100	622-121
GM F3	2379	57	N/A	2026-100	622-121
GM F3	2383	58	N/A	2026-100	622-121
	2056	52	2046W 6026W	2046-100	226E-92
Transfer Table	350	57	N/A	350-100	622-121
Coal Loader	397	48	N/A	397M-1	622-121
Coaling Station	497	53	N/A	497	622-121

UNIT #		Spring #	Bulb #	Volts	Roller #
GM F3	2363	622-191	1445	18	2367-192
GM F3	2368	622-191	1445	18	2367-192
GM F3	2373	622-191	1445	18	2367-192
GM F3	2378	622-191	1445	18	2367-192
GM F3	2379	622-191	1445	18	2367-192
GM F3	2383	622-191	1445	18	2367-192
	2056	2036-151	1445	18	2035-140
Transfer Table	350	622-191	N/A	N/A	N/A
Coal Loader	397	622-191	N/A	N/A	N/A
Coaling Station	497	622-191	N/A	N/A	N/A

	UNIT #	E-Unit	Smoke	Power Truck #
GM F3	2363	100-5	N/A	-
GM F3	2368	100-5	N/A	-
GM F3	2373	100-5	N/A	-
GM F3	2378	100-5	N/A	-
GM F3	2379	100-5	N/A	-
GM F3	2383	100-5	N/A	-
	2056	100-25	671-225	-
Transfer Table	350	N/A	N/A	-
Coal Loader	397	N/A	N/A	-
Coaling Station	497	N/A	N/A	-

CHAPTER ELEVEN
Fairbank Morse Diesel

UNIT #	Year	Tender #	Motor #	Brush #
F-M 2321	54	N/A	2321-100	622-191
F-M 2331	55	N/A	2321-100	622-191
F-M 2341	56	N/A	2321-100	622-191

Notes:

Notes:

UNIT #	Spring #	Bulb #	Volts	Roller #
F-M 2321	622-121	57	12-16	681-15
F-M 2331	622-121	57	12-16	681-15
F-M 2341	622-121	57	12-16	681-15

UNIT #	E-Unit	Smoke	Power Truck #
F-M 2321	100-7	N/A	-
F-M 2331	100-7	N/A	-
F-M 2341	100-7	N/A	-

Notes:

CHAPTER TWELVE
GP7 - GP9 Diesel

	UNIT #	Year	Tender #	Motor #	Brush #
EMD GP7	2028	55	N/A	2028-100	622-191
EMD GP7	2328	55	N/A	2028-100	622-191
EMD GP7	2337	55	N/A	2028-100	622-191
EMD GP7	2338	55	N/A	2028-100	622-191
EMD GP7	2339	57	N/A	2028-100	622-191
EMD GP9	2348	58	N/A	2028-100	622-191

Notes:

Notes:

UNIT #	Spring #	Bulb #	Volts	Roller #
EMD GP7 2028	622-121	57	12-16	2367-192
EMD GP7 2328	622-121	57	12-16	2367-192
EMD GP7 2337	622-121	57	12-16	2367-192
EMD GP7 2338	622-121	57	12-16	2367-192
EMD GP7 2339	622-121	57	12-16	2367-192
EMD GP9 2348	622-121	57	12-16	2367-192

Notes:

CHAPTER THIRTEEN
Rectifier Electric

UNIT #		Year	Tender #	Motor #	Brush #
GE E-33	2329	58	N/A	2028-100	622-191
GG1	2330	50	N/A	622-100	622-191
GG1	2340		N/A	622-100	622-191
GG1	2360		N/A	622-100	622-191
GG1	2332	47-49	N/A	2332M-1	2020M-33
EMD F3	2333	48	N/A	2333M-1	2020M-33
GE EP5	2350	56	N/A	2028-100	622-121
GE EP5	2351	57	N/A	2028-100	622-121
EMD F3	2352	58	N/A	2028-100	622-121
GE EP5	2358	59	N/A	2028-100	622-121
Gang Car	50		N/A	50-96	1661E-29

UNIT #	Spring #	Bulb #	Volts	Roller #
GE E-33	2329	622-121	57	12-16	2367-192
GG1	2330	622-121	1445	18	2330-18
GG1	2340	622-121	1445	18	2330-18
GG1	2360	622-121	1445	18	2330-18
GG1	2332	2020M34	1456	16-18	671-111
EMD F3	2333	2020M34	1445	18	622-138
GE EP5	2350	622-191	57	12-16	2328-173
GE EP5	2351	622-191	57	12-16	2328-173
EMD F3	2352	622-191	57	12-16	2328-173
GE EP5	2358	622-191	57	12-16	2328-173
Gang Car	50	WS-147	N/A	N/A	2033-43

	UNIT #	E-Unit	Smoke	Power Truck #
GE E-33	2329	100-4	N/A	-
GG1	2330	100-25	N/A	2330-25
GG1	2340	100-25	N/A	2330-25
GG1	2360	100-25	N/A	2330-25
GG1	2332	2332M-10	N/A	2332-20
				2333-153
EMD F3	2333	2333-80	N/A	2334-21
GE EP5	2350	100-4	N/A	-
GE EP5	2351	100-4	N/A	-
EMD F3	2352	100-4	N/A	-
GE EP5	2358	100-4	N/A	-
Gang Car	50	MECH	N/A	-

UNIT #	Year	Tender #	Motor #	Brush #
Fire Fight 52	58	N/A		622-121
ACC Switcher 57		N/A	41-80	622-121
Trolley 60		N/A	60-65	1661E-29
Maint Car 69		N/A	50-96	1661E-29
Burro Crane 3360	56	N/A	3360	622-121
Track Clean 3927	56	N/A	3927	622-121
R. C. Crane 182		N/A	182	
Mobile Rocket 44		N/A	44	
Launcher 45		N/A	45	
Portal Crane 282	54	N/A	282-100	622-121
Bascule Bridge 313		N/A	313	

	UNIT #	Spring #	Bulb #	Volts	Roller #
Fire Fight	52	622-191	57	12-16	41-22
ACC Switcher	57	622-191	N/A	N/A	41-22
Trolley	60	WS-147	432	12	41-22
Maint Car	69	WS-147	N/A	N/A	2023-43
Burro Crane	3360	622-191	N/A	N/A	2328-95
Track Clean	3927	622-191	N/A	N/A	2328-95
R. C. Crane	182		1456	18	
Mobile Rocket	44		19	14	
Launcher	45		19	14	
Portal Crane	282	622-191	N/A	N/A	
Bascule Bridge	313		N/A	N/A	

UNIT #		E-Unit	Smoke	Power Truck #
Fire Fight	52	MECH	N/A	-
ACC Switcher	57	100-6	N/A	-
Trolley	60	MECH	N/A	-
Maint Car	69	MECH	N/A	-
Burro Crane	3360	MECH	N/A	-
Track Clean	3927	MECH	N/A	-
R. C. Crane	182		N/A	-
Mobile Rocket	44		N/A	-
Launcher	45		N/A	-
Portal Crane	282		N/A	-
Bascule Bridge	313		N/A	-

Notes:

CHAPTER FOURTEEN
Locomatives

	UNIT #	Year	Tender #	Motor #	Brush #
Hudson	646	54-56	2046W	2046-100	226E-92
Hudson	2046	50-51 53	2046W	2046-100	226E-92

Notes:

Notes:

UNIT #	Spring #	Bulb #	Volts	Roller #
Hudson 646	2036-157	1445	18	2035-140
Hudson 2046	2036-157	1445	18	2035-140

Notes:

CHAPTER FIFTHTEEN
Whistle

	UNIT #	E-Unit	Smoke	Power Truck #
Hudson	646	100-25	671-225	-
Hudson	2046	100-25	671-225	-

Notes:

References

Lionel Factory Bulletins and Exploded Parts lists, 1949-1969

Greenberg's Repair and Operating Manual for Lionel Trains, 1945-1969, Pauker and Greenberg, Greenberg Books/ Division of Kalmbach Publishing Co   , ISBN: 0-89778-040-X, 1990

Printed in the United States
212547BV00003B/1/P